Truth Lives

Mary Ellen Ciganovich

Truth Lives

By Mary Ellen Ciganovich

Printed with Conversations Media Group

© 2021 by Mary Ellen Ciganovich

Cover design: DW's Simple Graphic Designs

Cover artwork: "Let Us Begin Again"
by Mr. Dino Carbetta

All rights reserved solely by the author. The author guarantees all content is original and does not infringe upon any other person or work. No part of this book may be reproduced in any form without the permission of the author except in the case of reviews or references by publications.

Printed in the United States of America

All Rights Reserved.

Acknowledgements

There are so many people in my life who have and continue to uplift, inspire, and push me to be my best version of myself. I wish to thank the following people for inspiring me to continue to inspire YOU!

Peter Ciganovich, you are a blessing in my life. God brought us together to enjoy His wonderful world as we learn from each other. As you once told me, "The best is yet to come." I look forward to each and every day loving you.

Stephanie, you are a gift God blessed upon me and our world. You inspire many people through your medical expertise and your many mountain climbing adventures. You amaze me, inspire me and I am proud to be your mother!

Cyrus Webb and the entire Conversations Media group: I cannot thank all of you enough for the many blessings you bring into my life. You and your wonderful friends add a boost of positivity to our world. For your friendship, support, and tremendous opportunities I will be forever grateful.

Mr. Dino Carbetta, a person I have never met yet he inspires many people through his Christian paintings. The cover of "Truth Lives" is from a painting Mr. Carbetta painted entitled, "Let Us Begin Again." Although Dino Carbetta does not usually allow his beautiful artwork to be used in this way, he was gracious enough to allow me to use "Let Us Begin Again" as the cover of "Truth Lives."

Table of Truths

1. Asleep or Awake
2. One Finger out…
3. Love Conquers fear
4. Respond to a situation
5. Take No thought
6. The problem is…
7. Change is inevitable
8. You are one with the natural world
9. Live Life with an open heart
10. Feel Comfortable with yourself
11. Say "yes" to you
12. Keep hope alive
13. Live an authentic life
14. Consistently improve yourself
15. Create positive change
16. Inspire with praise
17. Keep your thoughts focused

Table of Truths

18. Let go and stay now
19. Make change work for you
20. There is no Truth in "if only"
21. Do what excites you
22. Take time before making a big decision
23. Allow hope to guide you
24. Stay positive and upbeat
25. Let go of judgements
26. Worry is a no thing, a Nothing
27. Acknowledge your feelings
28. We are All Equal
29. Remove clutter
30. Act and make a difference
31. Appreciate your self-worth
32. Make your life an adventure
33. Achieve your goals

Table of Truths

34. See beyond the ordinary
35. Believe in your success
36. Create a sense of peacefulness
37. You create your experiences
38. Your health is your responsibility
39. You are stronger than you believe
40. Use active listening skills
41. Make a wish
42. Your choices impact others
43. Allow your natural self to shine
44. Be a source of inspiration
45. Make room for abundance
46. You are worthy
47. Connect to timeless wisdom
48. Be open minded
49. Give back to the world

Table of Truths

50. Your "knowing's" carry your Truth
51. You exist in a State of Grace
52. Overcome Limiting Behaviors
53. A Bright Future
54. Follow your heart
55. A True act of giving
56. Your spirit is eternal
57. Give positive reinforcement
58. Peaceful and patient mindset
59. Be the change you want to see
60. Make a decision
61. Forgive and let go
62. Find your own path
63. Get out of your own way
64. Take command of your life
65. Bless everything

Table of Truths

66. Your past is your teacher
67. True beauty comes from within
68. Communicate honestly
69. Possibilities are endless
70. Relationships are opportunities
71. Imagine yourself in the other person's shoes
72. Be of service
73. Practice Mindfulness
74. Honesty creates harmony
75. Choose to be non-judgmental
76. Choices and actions create your future
77. Emotion is the bearer of wisdom
78. Come from love
79. Forgiveness is a healing tool

Table of Truths

80. Raise your awareness level
81. Learn simplicity, patience, and compassion
82. Like-Minded people
83. Share Happiness
84. No Assumptions
85. Worry is an extension of fear
86. Progress is made through change
87. Face your emotions
88. Align your energy
89. Experience teaches wisdom
90. Take action to make your life work
91. Live in the moment
92. Notice your thoughts
93. Make your community better
94. Balance your obligations
95. Let go of little things

Table of Truths

96. Create unlimited possibilities
97. Let go
98. Grief is part of the Human experience
99. Be open to receive
100. Be delighted
101. Connect with your inner self
102. Choose an attitude of joy
103. Overcome Challenges
104. You are love
105. Learn and Grow
106. Empower yourself to lead
107. Treat yourself with care
108. Be honest with yourself
109. Be passionate about living
110. Make your movements mindful
111. Feelings are not permanent

Table of Truths

112. Choose, learn, and choose again
113. Connect to God's Laws of Truth
114. Explore your past to navigate your future
115. Elevate your consciousness
116. Your words are powerful
117. Center yourself
118. Sensitive moods cause anger
119. Organize your thoughts
120. Happiness is possible

A personal note from Mary Ellen

**About the Author –
Mary Ellen Ciganovich**

Introduction

"Truth Lives" is a book written to motivate, inspire and encourage all people throughout the world to live a life based on TRUTH. Not lies or facts you "think" are real – REAL TRUTHS! Truth never deviates or misleads you. These truths when applied daily to your life will assist you to create the peaceful, loving, and successful life you were born to live. I use these Truths daily in my own life. Living in Truth is not easy as your ego, your erroneous societal teachings and other worldly trappings deceive you and attempt to drag you down. I know! I have been down on the ground crying for God to rescue me so many times! Truths, handed down for centuries from one culture to the next are in our world so we can all live in love, harmony, and peace with each other.

Stay humbled as you awaken to live a loving Truth filled life. All Truths are born out of love and is the only thing that shall never die.

Thank you for supporting my work of encouraging, inspiring, and motivating all people to live their life based on Truth.

Sincerely with Love,

Mary Ellen Ciganovich

www.askmaryellen.com

Only love is Real
Nothing unreal exists
Herein lies the peace of God
Herein lies the peace for
All of humanity

Sincerely with Love,
Mary Ellen Ciganovich

1

Are you asleep or awake?

All of us "think" we are awake. All of us "think" we sleep only at night. I propose the theory many people, if not most people, live their life asleep!

They are asleep to the truth about themselves, yet they can see it so clearly in other people! They struggle through life going from one problem to the next as they tell themselves, "I can't help it" or "it's not my fault they made me do it."

What "asleep" people do not realize is all the "problems" or as I say "misperceptions, they go through are of their own making! It is the same problem just in a different form. Why do you give your power away to someone else? Probably so you can say it is their fault when things do not work out!

When you want your life to work you will wake up to your truth, let go of other people's motives, judgments or expectations and forgive yourself for any past errors.

It is my wish "Truth Lives" will help you do just that wake up from your negative, complaining, judgmental, worrisome, anxiety filled, stressed out life to see all the beauty life has waiting for you.

Let us all go forward to make our world a better place.

Now your Truth journey begins!

Enjoy the day.

Mary Ellen Ciganovich www.askmaryellen.com

2
One finger out – three pointing back!

Becoming aware is always the first step on your truth journey. This type of awareness I call "Awareness of Self." Awareness is your key to ignite that spark within you toward becoming all God wants you to be in our world. "Awareness of Self" of yourself is crucial and without completing this step you will stay stuck.

The easiest way to become aware of yourself is through a theory I learned as, "one finger out you have three pointing back." When you point a finger at someone else there are always three pointing back at you.

Meaning, the good you see in others is the good you have inside yourself and conversely the things about other people that irritate you are God's way or the Universe's way of showing you what you need to work on in yourself.

The good you see in others you should always bless as this goodness is in you. When you see something in another person that irritates, you or totally hooks you, step back to look at yourself. Understand there is something you need to learn? The other person probably is behaving badly and if it hooks you and you are bothered by what they did - day after day after day - it makes you angry or affects your life. My question to you is," why are you seeing it this way or what do you still need to learn?

Today become aware there is always something to learn!

Enjoy the day.

Mary Ellen Ciganovich www.askmaryellen.com

3
Love conquers fear

In Truth, there are only two emotions: Love or Fear.

You have been taught, erroneously, there are tons of emotions from happiness, joy, surprise and calmness to rage, anger, jealousy, and resentment. All your positive emotions come from the loving place within you. All your negative emotions come from your fear-based mind-set.

These fear-based thoughts, words, and deeds you are taught day by day, through what you read or watch, need to be discarded or they will flourish like weeds! Focusing on any fearful emotion such as worry, stress, anxiety, anger, negativity or complaining will not help any situation to be better. It will however make things worse or make you sick. Being stuck in fear breeds more fear, more negativity, more of everything you DON'T WANT!

The good news is your loving emotions should be fertilized and cultivated so they can grow stronger with each passing day. As you focus on your loving positive thoughts and emotions you draw more love into your life. You begin to open opportunities in your life for everything you DO WANT!

Today come from a loving heart, loving attitude, and loving mind as you drop any of your fears.

Enjoy the day.

Mary Ellen Ciganovich www.askmaryellen.com

4
Always Respond to a situation

To any situation or person, take time to respond out of love rather than reacting out of fear. You do not have to agree with what is being presented to you. Always have enough respect for yourself and the other person to address them kindly as you state your opinion.

How many times have you reacted to what someone said or did then later came back to apologize? You assume this about the person, or you assumed that about the situation and instead of taking a moment to respond, your ego pushes you to jump in with your immensely powerful and usually incorrect opinion. Think before you speak is a powerful rule of thumb to go by in life.

If someone comes at you from a fear-based tone, yelling, screaming, insulting etc. Stop and say to them, "what I need for me from you is _____" to stop yelling and calm down or just take a break so we may speak as adults.

If they continue in their negative fear-based way, then you must walk away until the person is ready to speak.

Today practice responding out of love.

Enjoy the day.

Mary Ellen Ciganovich www.askmaryellen.com

5
Take No Thought

Thoughts are things. They contain a certain amount of electrical energy. Successful people focus on thoughts to bring opportunities for success into their lives. If you are a person who focuses on negativity or what you do not want to come into your life - you are giving energy to creating exactly what you don't want!

The key to reprogramming your brain is through your thoughts. Your thoughts are the driving force behind the software your brain uses daily. As you raise your children, and they hear negative comments they turn these into thoughts. Your children then repeat these negative words to themselves. You are programming your children to have a negative outlook on life. When you say positive words to your children and you repeat them, you are programming your children to have positive thoughts in their future.

Your brain will deceive you unless you reprogram it. You fabricate your reality through your thoughts. It is important to wire your brain for success through positive thoughts. Self-talk is an important part of programming or reprogramming your brain. As are affirmations. You must be aware of the thoughts running through your brain. Choose to actively reprogram your brain by choosing different thoughts! When a negative thought comes back to haunt you, visualize a powerful positive thought pushing it out of your mind and destroying it.

Today be aware of all your thoughts because to change your life you must change your thoughts!

Enjoy the day.

Mary Ellen Ciganovich www.askmaryellen.com

The problem is You see a problem

In truth, there are no problems. There are perceptions and misperceptions. To the extent you see something as a problem, or misperception, you need to step back and ask yourself," how can I see this differently"? "What am I supposed to learn from this situation"? When you see a misperception in your life you can solve the "problem," or you can stay stuck. Problems are described as obstacles individuals have throughout their lives. Different "problems" present various levels of difficulty. Negative thoughts are misperceptions. You can choose to have problems in your life, or you can see them as misperceptions and learn to see things differently.

Today see any problem in your life as a simple misperception as you learn from it.

Enjoy the day.

Mary Ellen Ciganovich www.askmaryellen.com

Change is an inevitable truth

Change happens, so make change work for you. As you experience change in your life, control your response to the change that is in front of you. Change and the circumstances surrounding it can be a source of joy or a source of great stress and frustration.

The only truth about change is the fact that it is unavoidable. Instead of resisting change regard it as an opportunity to gain experience. Choose to make change work in your favor. Accept the fact you cannot hide from change. These "life changes" happen to you as they also continue happening all around you. You cannot stop or control change. You just need to open your eyes to the hidden blessings and opportunities hiding within these "life changes."

Optimism, enthusiasm, and flexibility will aid you in dealing with change as there is nothing to be learned by dwelling on what might have been or what might be in the future.

Focus on all the blessings coming to you during this time of change. Realize, "the best is yet to come."

Today become willing to embrace change with an attitude of positivity.

Enjoy the day.

Mary Ellen Ciganovich www.askmaryellen.com

You are one with the natural world

At the moment of your birth, you are perfectly attuned to the natural world. As time passes, you discover the sights smells and sounds of the materialistic synthetic world. These dazzle you and dim the memory of your naturalness.

You must become aware to bring your "naturalness" back to the forefront of your mind. As you go outside to connect with nature, breathing in fresh air, walking in the woods, or simply being at peace in nature through a "nature meditation" your level of wellness skyrockets.

I know you understand your body is not composed of plastics or other synthetic chemicals. When you consume fresh food, exercise correctly and breathe in fresh air you will stay healthy.

Of course, all bodies are different and when you do not eat enough healthy food some herbs or vitamins may be necessary.

Today rediscover the world of nature.

Enjoy the day.

Mary Ellen Ciganovich www.askmaryellen.com

Live life with an open heart

Spiritual teachers have always pointed to the heart as your "seat of consciousness." Approaching life with an open heart means you open your consciousness to a greater awareness. Doing this is as simple as shifting your attention onto your heart. When you make this a habit you can shift your attention to your heart center anytime you feel worried, stressed out, or in fear.

Simply sit with your eyes closed and draw your breath into your heart. As your breath expands your chest cavity expands, your heart expands and unleashes all your emotions. You may feel sadness, tenderness or relief as your emotions are healed.

Today open your heart to life's greatest treasures of calmness, compassion, and unconditional love.

Enjoy the day.

Mary Ellen Ciganovich www.askmaryellen.com

Feel comfortable with yourself

When you express your ideas do it with passion and conviction. This will make you feel more comfortable with yourself as you become assertive. If you have been harboring an idea, use this day to solidify the details.

Nurturing your confidence gives yourself courage to share these ideas with others. Expressing your confidence through being daring and bold, as you approach people, gives you the courage you need to succeed. Guidance from trusted friends reinforces your self-confidence. Feel more comfortable with yourself as you realize your full potential. Now, you can begin passing your ideas back and forth with those who are knowledgeable or can help you to clarify your plans.

Today feel comfortable with yourself as you go forward to achieve your life purpose.

Enjoy the day.

Mary Ellen Ciganovich www.askmaryellen.com

11
Say "Yes" to you

Recognizing the importance of "time for yourself" is far easier than finding time to take care of yourself. Every one of you has a "well of energy" inside that must be regularly replenished.

When you function as if you have a bottomless pit of energy, doing errand after errand, scheduling activities for every minute of the day, you become exhausted, weak, and open yourself up to a variety of illnesses.

Saying "yes" to you may mean you have to say "no" to someone else. It is one of the best things you can do for you and your family. You cannot take care of anyone else unless you take care of yourself first. People may say this is selfishness. This is the opposite of selfishness! You can excel in your outer world only if your own needs are met.

Today recognize the importance of "you time."

Enjoy the day.

Mary Ellen Ciganovich www.askmaryellen.com

Keep hope alive

Hope as you use it through your optimistic attitude, is a powerful force that contributes to your positive expectations about your future. Optimistic feelings, and feelings of hope, are your fuel aiding you to create positive energy. This powerful energy attracts more opportunities for success.

You can assist this process by consciously focusing on hopeful outcomes for any project you may have in front of you. When a negative thought creeps into your mind, visualize pushing it out with a positive one. As you get in the habit of replacing negative thoughts with positive ones your optimistic, hopeful outlook becomes stronger.

With new determination and a strong optimistic outlook, you gain focus and add strength to your intentions.

Today keep a positive and optimistic outlook regardless of any challenges you might face.

Enjoy the day.

Mary Ellen Ciganovich www.askmaryellen.com

13
Live an authentic life.

Your "true Self" exists and is sometimes buried under fears or learned behavior. This "true Self" is an elusive concept as most of you define your "self" by the roles you play throughout life. Your "Self" is further hidden by the fact society prompts you to suppress your intelligence, your uniqueness, your emotional and spiritual brightness.

In truth, you are all "light beings" in a physical body. Your true 'Self" exists whether you acknowledge it or not. My hope is that all of you will bring your light forward as you stop burying your light under fears and negative societal teachings.

Today shine your incredibly special and unique light upon the world.

Enjoy the day.

Mary Ellen Ciganovich www.askmaryellen.com

Consistently improve yourself and your circumstances

When you consistently improve yourself and your circumstances, your process of growth is enhanced. It is easy to just "ride the tide" of where you are now, especially if you are somewhat successful.

When you seek opportunities to keep improving yourself, and your circumstances, you continually create more abundance. Through continued improvement of yourself you become more self-confident. This brings new opportunities you "know" you can accomplish. Rather than strive to maintain where you are, ask other trusted people how you might improve.

With your focus on improvement, you not only deepen your relationship with yourself, you also begin a deeper relationship with loved ones.

Today focus on continued improvement.

 Enjoy the day.

Mary Ellen Ciganovich www.askmaryellen.com

15

Create positive change through the words you choose

You create a positive change in your life through choosing words that will create a positive picture of life. Your tone of voice is a particularly important facet of conveying your words correctly.

As our society moves forward language must be examined for any phrases no longer serving society. Watch your language carefully for phrases like; boys will be boys, boys don't cry, he/she is a problem child or other phrases that may convey or have a negative effect. Children are especially sensitive to these negative phrases and many of us carry these negative scars into adulthood.

Our language is a critical area to begin creating any positive change. Your words have a "ripple effect" as they influence and inspire others.

People subconsciously notice the way others speak. Without even thinking about other people will choose to speak differently.

Today choose to create a positive change through the words you say.

Enjoy the day.

Mary Ellen Ciganovich www.askmaryellen.com

16
Inspire with praise

Make a point today to give encouragement and positive messages to people in your life. Take a moment to let at least one person know how much their support means to you. You can accomplish this through a phone call, a text message or uplifting email. By giving praise to another you recognize all the love, positivity, and goodness you have in your life. As you express a kind word to any person you are acknowledging the value in all people.

Because we are all interconnected, this kindness comes back to you as it spreads out into The Universe. You can be sure this "gift of praise" you gave to another will be forwarded from person to person. As you take time to motivate people through praise you begin a "ripple effect" that influences more people than you will ever realize.

Today understand you have the power to influence others in a meaningful and powerful way.

 Enjoy today.

 Mary Ellen Ciganovich www.askmaryellen.com

Keep your thoughts focused on the positive

Fixate your thoughts on all that is good and positive. This may be easier to do in the morning hours and as the day wanes on it is easy to become sidetracked by all that is irritating or frustrating.

To ensure you stay positive, take time to notice all the goodness you see in others. Your day will grow brighter as you share your positive comments whether on social media or in person. Positive thinking is easy to do when things are going right for you.

As a human you tend to focus on the negative which leads to lowering your spirit, adding negativity to your world. Try to focus your attention on topics to make people feel good. You can enjoy the satisfaction of knowing in some small way, either for yourself or someone else, you made the world better.

Today give a sincere compliment or say a kind word as you spread positivity.

Enjoy the day.

Mary Ellen Ciganovich www.askmaryellen.com

18
Let go and stay NOW

Being tense or impatient causes feelings of unease in your life. As you learn to surrender to a calm mind, realize things do not always go according to plan. God/ the Universe has a plan for you and possibly what you are "trying so hard" to push through is not part of God's plan.

Let go, take a break, and repeat the affirmation, "I surrender." Letting go of having to make your life a certain way will allow you to be present in your life as it is NOW! When you make surrendering or clearing your mind part of your mental routine you begin to realize your "thoughts" are the cause of all your struggles.

Today surrender to the present moment and savor the serenity that comes from simply being NOW!

Enjoy the day.

Mary Ellen Ciganovich www.askmaryellen.com

Make change work for you

As you experience change in your life you control your response to the change that is happening. Change and the circumstances surrounding it can be a source of immense joy or a source of great stress. The only truth about change is it is unavoidable.

Instead of resisting change, regard it as an opportunity to gain experience. Choose to make change work in your favor. Accept the fact you cannot hide from change. Life changes happen to you as they happen all around you. You cannot stop or control change.

Open your eyes to the hidden blessings and opportunities hiding within these changes. Optimism, enthusiasm, and flexibility will aid you in dealing with change as there is nothing to be gained by dwelling on what might have been or what might be.

Today become willing to embrace change with positivity.

Enjoy the day.

Mary Ellen Ciganovich www.askmaryellen.com

20
There is no Truth in "if Only"

People who are unhappy give reasons that begin with "if only" …. Reasons such as," if only I had a better car" or "if only I had a better job" or "if only I could lose some weight" or "if only I were younger." In other words, "if only" one or two things in your life would change everything would be great.

This is NOT true. You may dwell on one thing while the real reason for your unhappiness goes unrecognized and unaddressed. When you become aware of the cause of your discontentment, usually within yourself not with anyone else, all your surface concerns have a way of working out. You may need a new car and these surface concerns will not cure the deeper issue.

Stop focusing on external factors. You have created a pattern in your life where you "thought" you were dissatisfied with one thing while you are in "truth" dissatisfied with something else.

This pattern will keep happening to you time after time until you learn. The only person whom you can be dissatisfied with is you!

Today slow down, turn your attention within as you drop" if only" from your vocabulary.

Enjoy the day.

Mary Ellen Ciganovich www.askmaryellen.com

21
Do what excites you

Every human life has the potential to be thrilling and inspiring. Your life depends on you and the choices you make day by day. Every day can be rousing and exciting or boring and tedious. You create an exciting life by doing things that excite you whenever the opportunity arises.

Know what excites you and what you like to do. Your views of what fun is may change from year to year. As you make excitement part of daily life, you will be open to exciting opportunities as they present themselves.

If you are a person who tends to live practically, excitement may overwhelm you at first. To ease this feeling, try incorporating small, exciting moments into your daily routine. As you make choices to do more of what excites you, feelings of unease dissipate and optimistic opportunities for excitement are created.

Today do something – even something small – you find exciting and fun.

Enjoy the day.

Mary Ellen Ciganovich www.askmaryellen.com

22
Take time before making big decisions

When you have a life changing decision take some time to be quiet with God. Any impulsive feeling will lead you toward deciding recklessly.

Impatience is a culprit that can cause you to be reckless with your money, time, or relationships. Your big decisions especially in these categories must be thought through. Ask a trusted friend mentor or family member for advice. Remember to ask a person who does not have an ulterior motive in the outcome of your decision. Take time to consider all your options.

As you take your time deciding, you will feel confident when you make your final choice. This "gift of time" allows your choice to be calm and centered. All of the patience you exercise helps the decision you make to be the right decision for your better future.

Today take some time before making any big decision while you remember the final decision is always yours.

Enjoy the day.

Mary Ellen Ciganovich www.askmaryellen.com

23
Allow hope to guide you

Hope will guide you through all of life's challenges. Devote a portion of your daily mental energy toward envisioning the future all your efforts are will achieve for you.

As you concentrate on your future success, with a hopeful attitude, you become encouraged to face any daily challenges. You can overcome any form of adversity when you face these challenges with hope in your heart.

This soul deep optimism motivates you to progress forward. This positive outlook is a source of strength and energy enabling you to concentrate on your successful future. As you imagine the "sweet taste of victory," your daily difficulties no longer seem overwhelming.

Today allow hope to fuel your ambitions as you see any set back as a new opportunity to move forward.

Enjoy the day.

Mary Ellen Ciganovich www.askmaryellen.com

Stay positive and upbeat

Always maintain a positive, idealistic, and forgiving attitude toward life. When you scroll through the Internet share examples of compassion and kindness. Making the most of an upbeat outlook on life is as easy as stepping back to look at your life with self-assurance.

When you see anything negative in society you are seeing it to learn. Keep your eyes open to see all the greatness and beauty in our world. Be patient with your fellow human beings as you view their actions in a compassionate light.

Keep your visions of the future joyful as you go forward inspiring others through "living your best life." Think optimistically about the people and opportunities that have yet to cross your path. Set up these wonderful situations to aid you in your success.

Today and always look for the best in people and life.

Enjoy the day

Mary Ellen Ciganovich www.askmaryellen.com

25
Let go of Judgments

To judge is to think you are better than others. It is to believe you know what is right, and other people are wrong. It is a form of control you use, possibly, without even being aware of it.

Judgements are taught through the "erroneous societal" teachings you learn. None of us want to be judged by others. So, why judge one another? Are you even aware when you are judging someone?

I like to believe," every person is doing the best they can." It might not look like it to you. You do not agree with what they are doing yet in that moment in their life that was the best they could do. They lack awareness of what they are doing and are clueless as to how to change it. Hopefully, this person will learn and do better in the future.

How about you? Can you stop judging? Can you do better? Today be aware of anyone or any situation you judge.

Enjoy the day.

Mary Ellen Ciganovich www.askmaryellen.com

Worry is a no thing, a Nothing!

Worry is an extension of fear. It is a learned habit and can be unlearned. Worry is very draining, yet there are people who think they must constantly worry in order to be a good wife, husband, mother, boss, or any other type of good person. I am sure you know someone who is a chronic worrier.

Worry is a self-created state of needless fear. Why worry about a situation that hasn't happened and probably will not happen in the future? Take a look at anything you worried about in the past. Did worrying about it fix it, change it, or make it better? No! You probably developed a headache or a stomach pain from all the worrying.

The good news is you can change this "worry" habit. Instead of worrying use your imagination to visualize the best outcome. See the worrisome situation bathed in white light with Angels guiding the outcome. Today generate peace and well-being instead of worry.

Enjoy the day.

Mary Ellen Ciganovich www.askmaryellen.com

Acknowledge your feelings

As you name your feelings you tame your feelings. This allows you to respond appropriately. You retake control of your personal power through becoming courageous enough to say these feelings aloud.

When you understand the emotions, you can control them instead of allowing your emotions to control you. This empowers you to let go of any painful feelings as you shift to a healing state.

Move past any apprehension you associate with expressing your distressing feelings out loud. You will become surprised to discover how liberated and lighthearted you feel.

Today give voice to your feelings, especially the negative ones, as you let them go.

Enjoy the day.

Mary Ellen Ciganovich www.askmaryellen.com

We are all equal

When you understand, "we are all equal" and "we are all connected" to source (God) you will see there is nothing lacking in your life. You understand we are All part of a "Higher Power." Whether you call this "Higher Power" God, or any other name is irrelevant because All of us have a part of this "Higher Power" within us.

Once you understand this concept you will let go of your need to compare your life to anyone else's life. Material resources are superficial and outer appearances do not signify fulfillment. Comparing yourself with others results in a feeling of lack.

When you look inside to what truly gives you value, you discover the wholeness we All share as we are All connected.

Today look inside to find your 'Higher Power" as you keep yourself connected, balanced and equal.

Enjoy the day.

Mary Ellen Ciganovich www.askmaryellen.com

Remove clutter and excess from your surroundings

A calm flow of energy encourages feelings of serenity. Remove any clutter or excess from your surroundings to begin a feeling of calm to flow through your home.

All of us go through times when we desire to purchase items and too many of them create feelings of stagnant energy. When an item no longer serves it becomes part of a disorganized, cluttered lifestyle. This leads to stagnant energy which can cause feelings of depression or fatigue.

Clear your surroundings, donating or giving items to others, gives freedom to a flow of abundant energy. It improves your mental, emotional, and physical health. The luxury of "things" you think you crave can instead be created through kindness, compassion, encouragement, and love as you clear your surroundings and reconnect with others. Today organize and clear any unnecessary clutter.

Enjoy the day.

Mary Ellen Ciganovich www.askmaryellen.com

Act on your desire to make a difference

It doesn't matter if you want to help the less fortunate or make progress in your own personal goals, the point is to take action. Let go of "staying stuck" and being ineffective. When you do something for someone else, you feel empowered and satisfied.

Give of yourself, your time, or your talents and any sense of depression lifts because YOU made a difference today. Be sure you are giving of yourself without expectations, motives, or judgements.

You will feel grateful for all the blessings in your life as you share your goodwill with others.

Today give of your time or other resources by asking where help is necessary and pitching in to do what you can to make a difference.

Enjoy the day.

Mary Ellen Ciganovich www.askmaryellen.com

Action may not always bring you happiness

And

There is NO happiness Without action

Sincerely with love,
Mary Ellen Ciganovich

Appreciate your self-worth

You are the only person who can validate your "sense of worth." Other people, with a low "sense of self" will attempt to bring you down. You are the only person responsible for your unconditional sense of worthiness.

Understanding it is not the other person helps you to understand your issues are self-imposed. You have the power to see things differently and do things differently. Learn what you need to learn from any situation, especially when dealing with difficult people.

At any moment you are free to choose an improved sense of self. Work hard, find supportive friends, and follow inspiring people. Let go of destructive relationships whether at work or home. Have faith in God, knowing you deserve better.

Today appreciate your sense of self-worth by knowing and making good choices.

Enjoy the day.

Mary Ellen Ciganovich www.askmaryellen.com

Make your life a great adventure of passion and joy

Your life will be a great adventure of passion and joy when you open your mind to exploring new ideas and experiences. A desire to break free from your usual routine is your signal you need more excitement in your life.

Make the choice to open your mind to innovative ideas, experiences, or opportunities for learning you add fresh energy to your life. This energizes and stimulates you. Every moment becomes an expression of passion and joy as you make continued choices to feel exuberant about your new life choices.

Today become free to pursue, learn about and participate in an activity that adds fun to your life.

Enjoy the day.

Mary Ellen Ciganovich www.askmaryellen.com

Achieve your goals

Having an optimistic attitude helps you to develop the perseverance you need to pursue your goals. It is easy to stay strong when things are going smoothly and when times are tough it is your attitude, your passion, your belief in your dream that propels you forward.

When you hit a rough patch, keep any challenge you face in in your mind as you manage it with an attitude of faith. Envision the challenge as a minor setback instead of a major obstacle.

This minor setback can now be overcome with your newfound momentum to move forward achieving your dream.

Today allow a lighthearted mood to push you through any challenges you may face.

Enjoy the day.

Mary Ellen Ciganovich www.askmaryellen.com

Gain a sharp vision, see beyond the ordinary

To create the life you want, see what is invisible to others. See not only "outside the box" see as if there is" NO box at all."

Be clear about what you want to create. Visualize everything down to the smallest of details or your wildest dream. Are you excited about it? Is this your passion?

Your vision must be connected with your passion, keeping you motivated, inspired, and excited about life. As you encounter challenges allow your vision to keep you going and on track. Share your "life vision" with trusted friends in order to inspire and motivate them on their life journey.

Your mind cannot tell the difference between what you imagine to be real and actual reality. This is why your thoughts and visions are such a crucial step in creating the life you want! Today take off your blinders and begin building your "life vision"

Enjoy the day.

Mary Ellen Ciganovich www.askmaryellen.com

Believe in your success

Developing a mindset of belief in your success triggers unconscious support programs in your brain to bring your goal to life. Your mind is now set up to give you an action plan to fulfill your dream.

Beliefs tend to change depending on time, place, and circumstance. Yet, a belief "mindset for success" will give you ideas and possibilities to overcome any obstacle.

You have been taught to trust your physical senses. Believe you can and will succeed goes beyond what your physical senses can perceive. A belief includes a doubt, yet a "mindset of belief" includes a knowingness in success. This type of belief, like faith, is based on knowing without evidence.

Today choose to believe {know} in your success as you allow God/The Universe to guide you.

Enjoy the day.

Mary Ellen Ciganovich www.askmaryellen.com

Create a sense of peacefulness

Let go of anything that drains you. Take a look at all the circumstances you put your energies into completing. Are these activities feeding your success or are they draining you?

Choose to sever your attachment to unnecessary personal or financial drains. As you make these choices, you create a sense of freedom and inner peace. With the absence of these draining circumstances, you create balance in your life.

Consciously choose which activities support your success and which activities to let go.

Today let go of draining circumstances as you create space for peace and balance.

Enjoy the day.

Mary Ellen Ciganovich www.askmaryellen.com

You are the creator of your own experiences

Life's many obstacles are there for you to learn from and to strengthen you. Become determined to push through them. It is easy for you to do this when you understand YOU are the creator of your experiences.

Focus on a positive outcome in all situations. Decide everything works out for your highest good. Now you have more positive energy to flow through your life. Shift your thoughts to match your desires.

During any challenging situation it is helpful to repeat an empowering affirmation such as," God/The Universe supports me in everything I do." Or "The Universe/ God is loving and nurturing."

Today boost your courage as you learn how to strengthen yourself to create the life experiences you deserve.

Enjoy the day.

Mary Ellen Ciganovich www.askmaryellen.com

Your health is your responsibility

Taking responsibility for your health assists you to become aware of the choices you make that contribute to your well-being. All of your choices are important to your health, from the thoughts you think, daily exercise you do or don't do and every food or drink you consume.

Your "TRUTHFUL" answers to these questions help you take responsibility for your health and form healthier habits. Positive healing energy begins to flood every cell in your being resulting in abundant health and wellness.

Today improve your health by seriously looking at your daily habits, foods you eat and anything else you may consume.

Enjoy the day.

Mary Ellen Ciganovich www.askmaryellen.com

You are stronger than you believe

You are always stronger than you believe. Negative emotions, fear, worry, stress, anxiety and many more, which keep you stuck cannot be dealt with until you change your thinking.

Recognize the futility of any unnecessary thought patterns. Find comfort as you redirect your attention to a deep breathing exercise. When you concentrate your thinking on something unrelated to your negative thoughts – something such as deep breathing, visualizations of success, any pleasurable pursuit or exercise – your negative thoughts dissipate. Meditation is also a useful coping mechanism as it provides a means to ground yourself in the NOW moment.

Today understand you are stronger than you think.

Enjoy the day.

Mary Ellen Ciganovich www.askmaryellen.com

Use active listening skills

Create a deeper level of communication as you strengthen your listening skills. Speaking kindly and respectfully is not enough if your attention is not on the words THE OTHER PERSON is saying to you. Never assume what another person is trying to convey to you. This is NOT listening.

Give your full attention to the conversation. Practice listening "beyond their words"! When you "listen beyond the words" you will understand the true intent of the message being said to you. Check out what you "think" you heard by rephrasing it back to the other person. This lessens the possibility of having a communication misunderstanding.

Most people are not listening. They are thinking about what they will say next to defend their point. If you think, someone is not listening to you, take a break and resume your conversation at a later point. Or just agree to disagree. Today be thoughtful as you focus on utilizing active listening skills.

Enjoy the day.

Mary Ellen Ciganovich www.askmaryellen.com

41
Make a wish

You may think making a wish has nothing to do with Truth. Not so. When you make a wish you are placing this "wish" as a thought into your consciousness. Your wish tells God/The Universe exactly what you want in your life.

Wishing inspires you to be playful. It opens up opportunities and possibilities in your life for your wish to come true. Whether your wish comes true or not it is important to express your hearts desires to The Universe/God. With every wish you open an intention to create this new wish {thought} in your life.

There is something magical and innocent about making a wish. Although you may live in the world of adulthood, it is a wonderful feeling when you can become a kid again – even just for a moment.

Today or the next time you see a shooting star, give yourself permission to be a kid again – make a wish!

Enjoy the day.

Mary Ellen Ciganovich www.askmaryellen.com

Consider how your choices impact others

Recognize the decisions you make and every course of action you take affects another in some way. You can influence others effectively when you stop to consider your choices and what impact these choices may have on other people.

Other people may not realize your kindness, yet once understood it will is always appreciated. Your influence among other individuals will be perceived with an elevated level of respect. With this new level of confidence, the impact of your influence sets a good example for everyone.

Today choose your words and deeds with care as you serve to influence other people through your example of "mindful awareness" and focused consciousness.

Enjoy the day.

Mary Ellen Ciganovich www.askmaryellen.com

Allow your natural self to shine

Many people hide their "true" self while they try to become what they "think" the other person wants them to be. This deception never works because it is false and therefore can never last. The result is a short-term unsatisfying relationship.

Being yourself is the key factor in developing fulfilling relationships with like-minded individuals. As you allow your natural self to shine, people will be drawn to you because of who you are NOT what they would like you to be.

This foundation of your relationship is now built on "Truth," sincerity and a shared trust rooted at the soul level. If desired, you can enter into a long lasting, rewarding relationship.

Today allow other people to see the real you.

Enjoy the day.

Mary Ellen Ciganovich www.askmaryellen.com

44
Be a source of inspiration

Every one of you have the ability to be a source of inspiration for yourself and other people. An encouraging word or just being a supportive listener can make a profound difference in someone else's day.

Do not discount the fact you can be a source of wisdom as you give another person an insight to create a better life. When YOU live your best life, you inspire someone else to be their personal best. Anytime you inspire someone you uplift the collective energy for all of us.

Today be a source of inspiration.

Enjoy the day.

Mary Ellen Ciganovich www.askmaryellen.com

45

Make room for abundance

This may seem like an unusual Truth and when your house is cluttered, your drawers are stuffed, and you are busy from sun-up to sun-down how can God/The Universe send you more? You already have more than enough, and you do not have time for any kind of relationship.

Take time to review the various aspects of your life. Open your eyes to eliminate unnecessary objects or wasteful tendencies. Unsubscribe to unwanted emails. Quit paying for apps or memberships you no longer use. Look at your automatic payments and let go of those no longer necessary. Clear out your closets and drawers.

By clearing out these unused or unnecessary items you make room for newer, more beneficial circumstances, things, or even relationships to enter your life.

Free yourself from unneeded material objects or spending habits and your level of stress goes away. Now, abundance comes your way. Today focus on clearing out clutter to make room for abundance.

Enjoy the day.

Mary Ellen Ciganovich www.askmaryellen.com

You are worthy

You are worthy as you are a beloved child of God/ The Universe. You have value as a person. Yes, you may stumble and fall and when you know you're a worthy, not only as a human being, but as a blessed child of God you can go forward with hope, joy, and a heart full of love to achieve anything.

Your worthiness, God's love, is what you are made of in your soul. This gives you strength, courage, and belief to never give up. Your "knowingness" in your worth keeps you going and creates new opportunities for your continued success.

If you cannot recognize these opportunities, open your eyes as they are right in front of you as blessings from God.

Today know you are worthy as you show appreciation to God/The Universe for all of God's many opportunities and blessings.

Enjoy the day.

Mary Ellen Ciganovich www.askmaryellen.com

Connect to the Universal stream of timeless wisdom

Heighten your intuition, knowing's, to connect with your spiritual center. Find a quiet place to be alone and visualize releasing all thoughts from your mind. Reach deep inside yourself as you tap into the intelligent wisdom within your core.

When you strengthen your awareness to this connection, the power of Universal wisdom within you and your mind will be opened. Your intuitive senses become stronger.

Remind yourself, your level of wisdom is not limited to your physical body. You are already a spiritual being. You are interconnected to Divine wisdom which always speaks to you through your "core self." This ability to tap into your "Higher Consciousness" leads you to create a fulfilling life.

Today strengthen your intuition, knowing's, as you focus on spiritual clarity.

Enjoy the day.

Mary Ellen Ciganovich www.askmaryellen.com

Be open minded

You find as you become flexible to listening to others you have greater success in any relationship. This happens because people see you as being accommodating to any new ideas they may present.

When you hold onto your ideologies to strongly, it makes it difficult to listen and understand new ideas from other people. This does NOT make any person right or wrong. In Truth there is no right or wrong only Truth.

Communicating with another person, gives you a balance between what is important for you and what is important to the other person. It is always okay if you do not agree as long as you treat each other with respect.

Respectfully listen to each other without interrupting. Compromise is your key to any healthy interaction within a relationship.

Holding on to your ideas too strongly will eventually destroy any relationship. Today inhale as you loosen the grip of your opinions and ideas, then exhale as you become receptive.

Enjoy the day.

Mary Ellen Ciganovich www.askmaryellen.com

Give back to our world

A world that gives you so much should be taken care of and left with your positive footprint. Begin by seeking out opportunities to share your resources with others. Adopt a selfless approach to assist people in need.

Giving in the spirit of generosity helps you to focus on doing the best in your community with whatever resources are available to you. Do not think, egotistically, about how your "giving deeds" impact your standing. Instead, devote the entirety of your energies toward accomplishing this philanthropic opportunity. Your unique talents leave a positive footprint, if not in the world, then at least in your community.

Today give selflessly as you positively touch other people's lives.

Enjoy the day.

Mary Ellen Ciganovich www.askmaryellen.com

Your internal "core knowing's' carry your Truth

There will be times in your life when it seems like everything is falling apart. People die, a relationship crumbles, and even your once stable career is in shambles.

These external factors may shift and your internal "core knowing's" remain steadfast. Lean on your "core self". This is your opportunity to learn your true identity.

When you place your identity and "sense of self" on external factors you risk losing everything as external factors can and will change. As the external changes, you are given the opportunity to discover your power found in your true "sense of Self."

Your true "sense of Self" is your core connection to your "Higher Power" God/The Universe or whatever you wish to name it.

This core connection is never affected by any circumstances governing your physical reality. Your true Self, your Truth, never changes as it simply is Truth.

Today connect to your Truth through your "core Self.'

Enjoy the day.

Mary Ellen Ciganovich www.askmaryellen.com

You exist in a State of Grace

God's grace exists inside all of us. It is your inner beauty that radiates from within you. It touches everyone you meet. It is the unseen hand of God to lift you up at the exact moment you need it.

Grace is not based on worthiness, nor is it earned through good deeds. It is unearned favor, freely given, bestowed from God and available to everyone.

Grace is the rain bringing relief to drought ridden farms. It is the unexpected lead to your perfect job opportunity that comes from a stranger. Grace is what happens to you when your miraculously escape injury or illness.

Grace resides in love between people, the check that comes unexpectedly in the mail, the cozy comforts of home or the forgiveness you bestow on yourself and others.

Grace is the state you are in when you pause to "Be" in the moment. To accept Grace, all you have to do is open your eyes and choose it!

Today see, experience, and choose Grace everywhere you go.

Enjoy the day.

Mary Ellen Ciganovich www.askmaryellen.com

52
Overcome limiting behaviors

Are you struggling with feelings of lack, insignificance, irritation, anger, or any other negative feelings? You may not realize you are laboring under these negative self-perceptions. Your self-awareness level is low and you run on auto pilot allowing these limiting behaviors to control your behavior.

Take time to honestly assess yourself and your circumstances. Become aware of limiting beliefs and self-sabotaging behavior. You may even want to ask a trusted friend how they see you, making sure you listen to what may be an uncomfortable truth.

Disregard all fears about your abilities. Embrace nurturing beliefs in order to free yourself to be completely happy, purposeful, and fulfilled.

Today replace feelings of inadequacy with your true sense of empowerment as you remember you are a perfect child of God/ The Universe.

Enjoy the day.

Mary Ellen Ciganovich www.askmaryellen.com

Prepare for a bright future

Optimism is a powerful motivator when you create an optimistic attitude to visualize the fulfillment of your future dreams. As you approach your world optimistically, you will see a vast number of opportunities to lead you toward your goal.

Negativity convinces you there is little reason to even pursue your goal. As you go forward let any of these negative forces holding you back drop from your conscious awareness.

Create the belief you are capable of meeting and overcoming any challenge. This new optimistic attitude, fortified by your positive thoughts, creates your forward-thinking action you need to succeed.

Today be optimistic about your future.

Enjoy the day.

Mary Ellen Ciganovich www.askmaryellen.com

Follow the guidance of your heart

Life is always comfortable when you choose individuals whose values are similar to your own. Through being kind to all people you can expand your horizons and your ideas. Make a good impression by simply being yourself.

Try NOT to get caught up in the whims of a crowd. Be dedicated to YOUR convictions in order to show others it is your intention to live according to your values. These values you project appeal to others provided you are being true to your Higher Self. Your best self is always shown when you follow the guidance of your heart.

Today simply be yourself – first you must know yourself.

Enjoy the day.

Mary Ellen Ciganovich www.askmaryellen.com

A True "act of giving" lies in the value it has for both people

Keep in mind it is essential to ask the other person before you do things for them. You do not necessarily need to ask their permission. It depends on what you are planning to do for them. Make sure your help is really needed.

Never assume as 99% of all assumptions are false. Give or do for others out of a sense of true concern for their needs. It is important to be sure the other person wants or needs what you plan to do or give.

Some people support others because it enhances their own "sense of self-worth." This person considers themselves the "rescuer" and "thinks" the other person cannot survive without them.

Lend a hand because someone really needs it, not out of any sense of obligation.

Today remember a true "act of giving" lies in the value it has for both people.

Enjoy the day.

Mary Ellen Ciganovich www.askmaryellen.com

Your spirit is ever renewing, ageless and eternal.

Every one of you have a "spiritual self" that infuses your thoughts and feelings throughout the day. This "spiritual self" is not small or big it is both at the same time. Your individual spirit is like a drop in the ocean of the whole world's spiritual energy.

Your spirit inhabits your body similar to a passenger riding in a car. At the same time, your spirit is not bound by your body. How many times have you thought of someone when all of a sudden you hear from them? Spirits can reach across miles, time, and space to touch the heart of a loved one or friend.

Your spirit is ever renewing, ageless and eternal. This "spiritual self" is not old or new, big, or small. It is all of these at once. Your "spiritual self" connects you to your oneness and the changeless energy of our world. Today open yourself up to the fullness of your spirit.

Enjoy the day.

Mary Ellen Ciganovich www.askmaryellen.com

Give yourself positive reinforcement

When you experience feelings of discouragement or frustration, be gentle with yourself. Become inspired to continue pursuing your goals through positive reinforcement.

Unexpected obstacles will challenge your determination to succeed. Do not judge yourself, be critical of yourself or demand perfection. Take a break to give yourself some positive reinforcement.

You may want to repeat loving affirmations to encourage yourself to progress. The more you affirm your willingness to be patient, flexible, loving, and strong, the more strength you will find within yourself to overcome any obstacles. Your frustration, depression, and negativity lifts as you treat yourself with kindness.

Today make a choice to go easy on yourself as you create a positive state of mind.

Enjoy the day.

Mary Ellen Ciganovich www.askmaryellen.com

Surrender to a peaceful and patient mind-set

When you struggle with impatience you find yourself feeling stuck, frustrated, and unable to make positive changes in your life. A peaceful and patient mind-set provides the endurance you need to outlast any challenges you may face.

Focusing your mind on peacefulness and patience, regardless of what you may be going through, empowers you to stay balanced and optimistic. This gives you the strength you need to create determination and hope as any problems dissipate.

Today choose to surrender to a peaceful and patient mind-set in all your experiences.

Enjoy the day.

Mary Ellen Ciganovich www.askmaryellen.com

Be the change you wish to see

You can be the change you wish to see in your world when you change your perceptions to think creatively and do things differently. A change in your perspective and your behaviors moves you past life difficulties with minimal effort.

There are times in your life when you feel hopeless. You keep trying different ways to reach your goals and all have yielded fruitless results. As a human being it is in your nature to assume if you do it again and try just a little bit harder the outcome will be different. This is a huge falsehood! These behavior patterns that happen over and over again can be overcome when you wake up to your awareness of self.

It takes bravery and courage to question your behaviors, choices and change them. With diligence and hard work, you can use new innovative ideas to become the change you want to see in your world.

Today wake up to new possibilities as you step away from your circular path to explore an untried path of awareness.

Enjoy the day.

Mary Ellen Ciganovich www.askmaryellen.com

Make a decision

Any decision you make leads you to a greater understanding of yourself. The point is to MAKE A DECISION! Stop giving yourself reason after reason for having a life, job, partner, or anything else you DON'T want in your life!

Release your fear of the future by learning and accepting any past indecisive moments. Where did these "lack of decisions get you? Take a moment to think about the chances you didn't take. Not with regret, from a learning point of view. Regret immobilizes you just as much as fear. Both will keep you stuck.

When you look at any life experience as a lesson, to be learned from, you can realize any decision you made lead to a greater understanding of yourself.

Today let go of fear, regret or any other emotion that may be keeping you from making a decision as you realize everything in life is an opportunity for learning and growth.

Enjoy the day.

Mary Ellen Ciganovich www.askmaryellen.com

To understand Truth

sit in silence

As

the quieter you become

the more you hear

Sincerely with Love,

Mary Ellen Ciganovich

Forgive and Let Go

The first person you must forgive is yourself! Forgive yourself for following bad advice, expecting someone else to be the person they're not, and forgive yourself for harboring any motives, judgements, or expectations. When you hold onto any past grievance the only person you hurt is you!

Understand the Universe/God is trying to teach you through this "situation" or other person. Sit quietly to look back, visualize what happened, learn, and let go. Now, this past hurt can finally heal.

Once you begin to practice letting go and forgiving your past hurts, your energy will change. You feel lighter, more peaceful, and ready to live life to the fullest. Your relationships will become fulfilling as you are more fulfilled yourself. Any career potholes, or other issues, begin to turn around because you are becoming the loving, successful, peaceful person our society needs. Today forgive and let go!

Enjoy the day.

Mary Ellen Ciganovich www.askmaryellen.com

62
Find your own path

When you deal with people who are totally unaware, remember everyone must find their own way toward awakening. You may be aware we are all one, connected and emanate from the same Source – God. Wonderful! You are on your way toward understanding your awakened "true Self."

However, all people just don't get it. They probably never will. This is not right or wrong as in Truth there is no right or wrong – just Truth. You may find it frustrating to watch these people struggle through life, unconsciously aware of their truth.

It is easy for you to judge these people and become intolerant of them. It will help you to know even these "unaware" individuals are part of God's plan. When you find yourself "Awake" there are still places in your own mind and heart that need healing. Your journey is just beginning.

Our world is beginning to wake up. There are many dark places needing people to bring their love, forgiveness, kindness, inspiration, encouragement and healing.

Today understand the true healing of our entire world, our whole society depends on the awareness of each and every individual.

Enjoy the day.

Mary Ellen Ciganovich www.askmaryellen.com

63
Get out of your own way

It is amazing how often you get in your own way without being aware of what you are doing? You "think" you want to succeed yet you give yourself reason after reason to block your efforts.

Most of the time, people are not afraid of failure as we have all failed numerous times. You are afraid of success! Subconsciously you are afraid to succeed. Possibly, you make your goals so difficult that no person could ever achieve them. Or do you approach your goals in a way it keeps creating the same results over and over again?

If you think this describes you then you are standing in your own way. Do you really want to succeed? If so, write down all the choices you made so far toward achieving your dream. Write down the effort you put forth after making these choices. Are there any fears keeping you stuck? What prompted you to go in this direction? Are you passionate about completing this goal or is this someone else's dream for you?

Honestly answer these questions. Look at what you wrote down. Now go forward, change directions, or choose a different dream.

Today face any obstacles blocking you – let go to find success!

Enjoy the day.

Mary Ellen Ciganovich www.askmaryellen.com

Take command of your life

Take command of your life by feeling self-assured as you interact with other people. These uplifting, positive feelings encourage you to take risks in your personal and business activities.

While confidence is wonderful, make sure you demonstrate it in subtle ways. Come from your "God-driven core" not your ego "self." Weigh your words and actions before expressing yourself to others. Pause to consider the consequences and potential effect of your words or actions.

You can take command of your life and further your goals by taking other people's feelings into consideration while communicating. This behavior helps people to listen with respect, fall in line with your requests and achieve your success as you inspire others to also be successful.

Today cushion your authority while taking command of your life.

Enjoy the day.

Mary Ellen Ciganovich www.askmaryellen.com

Bless everything in your life

It is easy for you to feel good about yourself when success is visible on the horizon, and it is far more difficult when you are going through annoyances. Recognize how lucky you are to simply be alive. Bless everything in your life, from minor joys to any experience that makes you smile.

Every day as you wake up healthy and generally satisfied, count yourself lucky as you are far better off than much of humanity. As you grow in your appreciation of your small blessings, you will be abundantly blessed with larger ones.

Today feel prosperous and fortunate about your wonderful life as you count your many blessings.

Enjoy the day.

Mary Ellen Ciganovich www.askmaryellen.com

Your past is your teacher

To discover fresh insights about who you are delve deeply into the very core of your soul. Understand how your past has influenced your life. Look at, examine, explore, and learn from your past life experiences. Does your past sill have something to teach you? Is it influencing your present moment choices?

As you uncover lessons from your past you still need to learn, you empower yourself to be successful in the present. You rid yourself of any "excess baggage" keeping you stuck.

Through quiet meditation, as God speaks to you, the answers present themselves. These will be both eye opening and meaningful.

Today reflect on where you have been to understand where you are going.

Enjoy the day.

Mary Ellen Ciganovich www.askmaryellen.com

True beauty comes from within

True beauty is the person who shares a smile with a perfect stranger. Beauty comes from your heart, when you lend a helping hand to someone in need, listen to a friend in emotional pain, or give unconditionally.

Be committed to knowing and being your REAL authentic self. Become Aware! You are enough – Perfect- just the way you are NOW! If you are striving to be perfect, you are telling yourself you are not enough. Nothing could be further from your Truth!

You are amazing! Imperfections and all! Utilize your strengths to become vulnerable as you reach out to others for assistance. Stand strong in your beliefs while you allow other people to share their inner beauty with you.

Today know you are beautiful just the way you are as you share your inner beauty with the world.

Enjoy the day.

Mary Ellen Ciganovich www.askmaryellen.com

68
To build Truth communicate honestly

When you honestly communicate your feelings to others it leads to a greater sense of shared trust. Truthful communication promotes affection with loved ones. All of us like to hear, verbally, how much we are loved and appreciated. It can be difficult to say what is in your heart, yet when you do, you open your relationship up to a roadmap for success because you are sharing the purest and most render part of yourself.

All people, in Truth, are bound by love. This bond is something unlimited and unconditional. As you express these loving or kind feelings with yourself, family members or friends you deepen the relationship. This paves the way for a better relationship with open and honest communication.

Today make your communication and expressions of love clear and meaningful.

Enjoy the day.

Mary Ellen Ciganovich www.askmaryellen.com

Your possibilities are endless

Are you filled with idealism about the kind of future you want to create? Maybe you already know what you want to do in your personal, work, or spiritual life. You may just be starting the process of deciding what steps to take. All your possibilities are only as limited as you allow them to be.

Before you begin taking steps, create a clear vision of the life you want to create. Take time to sit down and write a list of goals. Now, write a list of possible actions you can take to meet your goals. Give yourself permission to write down any and all ideas that come to mind. Because anything is possible!

Today remember your possibilities are only as limited as you allow them to be.

Enjoy the day.

Mary Ellen Ciganovich www.askmaryellen.com

Relationships are opportunities for learning

Relationships are opportunities for you to learn to love yourself. The purpose of any relationship is to learn who you are, and whom you can become. A relationship should give you the freedom to learn the essence of "unconditional love". By having no motives, no expectations, and no judgements your relationship and what it "should be" you can learn "true love."

Rather than focusing on your differences – focus on your similarities as spiritual beings. If a relationship becomes fearful or dangerous – GET OUT – because you should always remain safe. Relationships should always be possibilities for love. Your life journey is all about learning to love yourself.

Today look inside yourself to see opportunities for love as first you need a loving relationship with you!

Enjoy the day.

Mary Ellen Ciganovich www.askmaryellen.com

Imagine yourself in the other person's shoes

Harmonious interactions begin by relinquishing your own needs and recognizing the needs of others. Conversations within relationships are not always easy or pleasant. Balanced discussions come from a point of middle ground with both people listening and learning from the other. Assess the needs of your friends or partners to be able to see your ideas are not always correct.

When you stubbornly refuse to see all sides of any issue you remain stuck in your "lack of understanding." Considering someone else's feelings and what is going on in their life makes it easier for you to understand issues from their point of view. This helps you smooth any friction that arise during your conversation.

Today take a deep breath as you imagine yourself in the other person's shoes.

Enjoy the day.

Mary Ellen Ciganovich www.askmaryellen.com

Be of Service

Be of service to those around you or humanity in general. Use your creativity and compassion to produce original ways to help. There are many organizations you can become a part of or assist through the use of your many talents.

You may wish to create a new organization to help our world. Begin a discussion group to involve more people to see if they have ideas. Lead the charge for change in your community. This need not be overwhelming. Begin small as you are the spark. All you need is an idea!

Today use your creativity and compassion to lead you to be of service.

Enjoy the day.

Mary Ellen Ciganovich www.askmaryellen.com

Practice the art of mindfulness.

Practicing the art of mindfulness allows you to experience every moment in a deep and profound way. When you practice mindfulness, outside in a natural setting, you feel the joy, harmony, and encouragement flowing through your wonderful world.

If you are too busy to notice these natural miracles during your daily activities, you end up feeling disconnected and empty. Then you wonder why you are full of stress, anxiety or worry.

During any mindfulness activity you become aware of your "True Spiritual Self." You allow your thoughts to float away. You drop all worries as you enjoy life on a meaningful level. Stay in this NOW moment to connect with your sense of joy.

Today focus on mindfulness as you intensify joy and happiness in your life.

Enjoy the day.

Mary Ellen Ciganovich www.askmaryellen.com

Honesty creates harmony

There is never anything to hide in a relationship or any interaction when you are honest. First, you must be honest with yourself.

Ask yourself the following questions: 1. Do you think before you speak? 2. Do you say one thing and mean what you say? Always following through with your actions 3. Do you communicate with others in an open and honest way? Are you sure the other person hears and understands you 4. Do you look at both sides of any situation?

Honesty is important. It is your internal regulator to keep you balanced. When you are out of balance you see your world off balance as well. Without balance, without harmony, without honesty you cannot have a healthy relationship with anyone even yourself.

Today choose to be honest with yourself as well as others.

Enjoy the day.

Mary Ellen Ciganovich www.askmaryellen.com

Choose to be non-judgmental

Open yourself up to individuals with widely differing points of view. Make sure you address them with respect and a sincere level of curiosity. The people you converse with will give you the same level of consideration when you express your ideas. Both of you need to appreciate the fact you have differing opinions or beliefs. This is not right or wrong – simply different points of view needing to be respected.

Your choice to be non-judgmental adds to your sphere of influence as people see you having respect for ALL people. This mutual respect and consideration you show others bridges the gap as you teach people, through your example, it is possible to interact peaceably. Even when you do not agree with each other!

Today learn how others think by respectfully asking questions and respectfully listening to their

answer.

Enjoy the day.

Mary Ellen Ciganovich www.askmaryellen.com

The choices you make and the actions you take today, create your future

Every choice you take either drives you closer to your goal or farther away from it. This does not mean every choice you make has to be correct. It does mean your actions and choices shorten your journey toward your goal or make it longer.

At times, I overhear people say they do not care about their choices because "God" will correct them and lead them to what is right. Well, God already did lead you to do what is right, why didn't you choose it? Why are you trying to sabotage your purpose? Yes, God can lead you and YOU must listen and follow Him.

Every choice you make is important from the moment you get up to the moment you fall asleep. Your choices throughout your day should be choices in alignment with your purpose.

Your choices are important and mean nothing without following up with actions. There are tons of people who will tell you, "Well I meant to ____." Meaning to do something is not doing it! Trying to be happy does not create happiness.

Today make a choice, follow it with action and get results.

Enjoy the day.

Mary Ellen Ciganovich www.askmaryellen.com

Emotion is the bearer of wisdom

You may "think" you have resolved your past issues. You did a lot of hard work learning to put these issues behind you. Now, they are gone! Or are they?

Think about a past issue something that really hooked you. Or think about a person you could not stand being around. Bring a picture of "the issue" or "the person" into your mind. Slowly, mentally, remove the emotional layers you feel. Name these emotions. Where are you feeling these emotions, in your gut, your head, your neck or feet? Allow these emotions to just be – respect these feelings even if you do not understand them.

What wisdom messages are coming to you? Hear it, feel it as this wisdom is coming to you from God/The Universe. Your soul and your knowing's are guiding you to a new level of awareness. Feel your emotions and let them go!

Today work through your emotions to gain wisdom.

Enjoy the day.

Mary Ellen Ciganovich www.askmaryellen.com

Always come from Love

You create more depth and meaning in your relationships when you choose to express love and care for others without expecting anything in return. It is always a wonderful feeling when your love is reciprocated. You will sabotage your relationship if you make this a condition of why you are expressing your feelings. Real love is always unconditional.

By choosing to share your love freely, regardless of the responses you receive, you feel fulfilled to freely express any emotion in your relationship. At the same time, you are encouraging others to open up to you. Understand every loving word and gesture contributes to the healing of our society.

Today express love, affection, and gratitude to all people in your life as you inspire others to do the same.

Enjoy the day.

Mary Ellen Ciganovich www.askmaryellen.com

Forgiveness is a healing tool

Your most powerful "heart" medicine is forgiveness. I am not speaking about forgiving others, although that an important part of any healing journey. The forgiveness you must practice is "forgiveness of self." This type of forgiveness teaches you to release your past as you learn from it.

"Forgiveness of self" allows you to let go of any mistakes or errors in judgements you might have made in life. This forgiveness of self teaches you to release your sadness and find gratitude for what you learned as you went through these errors. What good does it do to hold to your mistakes berating yourself for something that happened in the past?

Forgiveness brings you joy, freedom and a knowingness you are a perfect child of God/The Universe mistakes, and all. When you are by yourself, the power of forgiveness sends you love – the love of Self.

Practicing forgiveness both of others and "forgiveness of Self" releases you from pain, isolation, and fear. You now embrace all the love God has to offer.

Today forgiveness is your healing tool to slay fear and bring you back to love. Enjoy the day.

Mary Ellen Ciganovich www.askmaryellen.com

Raise your Awareness level

What you focus on expands and what you think about happens is a powerful Truth! Most people use this truth incorrectly. They will journal or even meditate for an entire day thinking about the life they want to create. The problem is there is no plan. They do not take opportunities when presented because they don't want to do the work. They like their reasons for staying in their world of lack.

Take all of these negative thoughts that do not ever work for you and visualize discarding them. Write them down and put them through a shredder or do some other activity to release them from your consciousness.

Raise your awareness level. Your awareness of Self! Create thoughts to bring your successful life into reality. Then be AWARE of the opportunities as they arrive. Become excited about life. Be enthusiastic as you practice gratitude every moment of every day. Gratitude like prayer needs to be practiced continually not only in moments of sadness or despair.

Raise your Awareness level to consciously see all that is right in your life. Bless every place, person, or situation for which you are grateful.

Today focus on your life as you want it to be and do the work to make it happen.

Enjoy the day.

Mary Ellen Ciganovich www.askmaryellen.com

In Life learn three things
Simplicity Patience Compassion

Simplicity, patience, and compassion are three life lessons you must learn to generate peace within you. These three attributes are interesting and hard to learn as the human "ego" will attempt to keep you confused struggling through life.

Simplicity is important. You always have everything you need when you need it. Why to do want more? Why do you have to have more? Be content with what you have now. Give to others this is how you give to yourself.

Patience with yourself is important. Have patience to allow God/The Universe to work through you. Practice patience with yourself. Practice patience with your friends and family. When you pray for patience be careful because God/The Universe will send you trials and tribulations to answer your prayers.

Compassion for yourself and others is a necessary attribute to have as it gives you sympathetic understanding of your suffering and enables you to be motivated to assist others to relieve their suffering.

Today accept your fellow humans the way they are as you achieve simplicity, patience, and compassion.

Enjoy your day.

Mary Ellen Ciganovich www.askmaryellen.com

Attract "Like-Minded" people

When you make the decision to change your attitude God/The Universe sets into motion "like-minded" people to come into your life. These "like-minded" people help you put the pieces of your life together. A sense of peace overcomes you and you KNOW all your dreams are possible.

This shift in your attitude, your mind-set, opens up brand new possibilities for you to explore. Your focus becomes clear, and you move forward with a strong level of confidence. This positive shift attracts like-minded people to you. It affects everything and everyone around you. Like a rush of water, it clears the debris from your path so you can move forward.

Today enjoy your new attitude as you attract like-minded people into your life.

Enjoy the day.

Mary Ellen Ciganovich www.askmaryellen.com

Share your happiness

Having fun and sharing a lighthearted mood should always be items you write on your daily "to do" list! Your desire to play and enjoy life, throughout your day, inspires other people to have fun.

Consider different activities you could do to bring your happiness forward. Invite someone to go for a walk, a hike, a cup of coffee or a fun activity at your home. As you are out during your day, and you feel like singing – sing! If you feel like dancing – dance! Drop any thought about not being "good enough." There is no right or wrong when it comes to having fun or being creative.

Creative activities are a wonderful way to express feelings of joy and fun. It doesn't matter if you "think" you can draw or not because it is not about the "art" it is about bringing your good emotions and feelings into the light. Today share your happiness as you engage in creative fun activities.

Enjoy the day.

Mary Ellen Ciganovich www.askmaryellen.com

Make NO Assumptions

You may "think" others are treating you badly or talking behind your back. You may believe people are judging you. Could it be your own feelings of self-consciousness you are experiencing?

Remind yourself, you cannot read other people's minds. Ninety-nine percent of ALL assumptions are false. You will improve your outlook on life by allowing other people to have their opinions.

Understand, every person you pass as you go about your day have their own issues and reasons for their behaviors. If you are having a bad day, it is easy to assume other people are forming opinions about you. Since you are feeling insecure, your own judgements and assumptions make you resentful around others.

Today remember what really matters is your goodwill and the unconditional love with no judgement, motives, expectations you show to other people and especially yourself.

Enjoy the day.

Mary Ellen Ciganovich www.askmaryellen.com

Worry is an extension of fear

During your life, I am sure you have experienced worrying. Some of you may even have the "worry" habit. You do not go through a day without dozens of worries. Worry is an extension of fear, it will drain your energy.

The main reason you worry is due to feeling a lack of control. Your children grow up, find a place of their own and you constantly worry if they are doing well on their own. You call, text or email and when you don't receive a response your "worry habit" Kicks in keeping you anxious, nervous, and wide awake.

There is a way to transform your "worry habit" into a habit of healing. When you worry you use your imagination to create the worst outcome for a given situation.

Your healing habit for worry is to use your imagination to visualize the best outcome!

Utilize your mind's eye to imagine Angelic guides watching over your loved ones or any situation you may be worrying over. Let go and give it to God/The Universe.

Today understand worrying about something never changes the outcome.

Enjoy the day.

Mary Ellen Ciganovich www.askmaryellen.com

Progress is made through change

Do you cling to certain ideas or commitments throughout your life? Is your mind closed off to any new ideas or ways of thinking? You can make this choice. Yet, as the years go by, and you change you will find your dedication to these ideas or commitment changing.

Change is a necessary element for personal growth. As you become flexible with your viewpoints, you see any challenge as a learning experience. Your mind-set will see these changes with positivity guiding you toward your destination. In order to make continued progress, analyze each situation for its unique set of life lessons.

Today question the value of being stuck to your ideologies as you accept that change is necessary for your progress and personal growth.

Enjoy the day.

Mary Ellen Ciganovich www.askmaryellen.com

Courageously face your emotions

Make peace with your negative emotions as you courageously confront them rather than running from them or hiding them in a misguided attempt at self-protection.

Your "human" initial response may be to withdraw from the source of tension these emotions bring up. What you do not realize is when you do not face your emotions and learn from these challenges, the same emotions will still be waiting for you when you surface from your isolation.

Gather your courage to confront your emotions straightforwardly. This allows you to empower yourself reestablishing peace and positivity within your consciousness. You begin to understand it is your misperceptions about life that brings these negative emotions to the forefront of your mind.

Today gather your courage to stand before any challenges or emotions you face.

Enjoy the day.

Mary Ellen Ciganovich www.askmaryellen.com

Align your Energy

Consciously harness the energy behind your thoughts and moods as this helps you to be productive. The energy within you is yours to direct at any time.

Energy is your power source to be channeled toward any activity requiring your attention. Your energy is yours to command or waste. It is always your choice!

When you sit around the house your energy becomes sluggish and your body responds with fatigue. As you make yourself move, your energy lights up producing increased energy and renewed enthusiasm.

Your energy is yours to command any way you wish.

Today direct your energy in ways to benefit you to feel centered, focused, and productive.

Enjoy the day.

Mary Ellen Ciganovich www.askmaryellen.com

Experience teaches wisdom

Your past teaches you to make better choices in the future ONLY when you learn from these past experiences. This level of awareness is one of your most helpful tools to learn about yourself. As you review your past become aware of how your choices, circumstances or behaviors led you to where you are now. Use this information and all the wisdom you gain to break any limiting behaviors you might still exhibit. Through gaining this wisdom you can make decisions in alignment with your future plans.

Every time you are faced with a new choice utilize this wisdom from past experiences to direct your decision. This "new" choice is coming to you because you can now see things differently. You have the wisdom you learned from your past experiences.

As you continue along your life journey you will have new experiences teaching you wisdom when you choose to learn.

When you learn you will become able to manifest your dreams as new opportunities are brought forward.

Today release old thought patterns as you gain wisdom through your experiences.

Enjoy the day.

Mary Ellen Ciganovich www.askmaryellen.com

Take action to make your life happen

Take some time to give thought to your dreams and goals. Outline the actions you can take to get the results you want. Write these down. During the course of your day look for opportunities to come your way. When you are presented with an opportunity, even if you are busy, take a moment to review it. Is it in alignment with your goals and values? If it is grab it with both hands.

Your enthusiasm to take these new opportunities leads you to achieve exactly what you want in your life. Now, increased opportunities come your way. As a result, achieving your goals becomes simpler and your journey towards success is shortened.

Today combine your ambitious attitude with a directed focus to take action to achieve your goals.

Enjoy the day.

Mary Ellen Ciganovich www.askmaryellen.com

Life either happens to you or you take hold of life with both hands and Live it!

Sincerely with love,
Mary Ellen Ciganovich

Live in the moment

Life, in all of its beauty and fullness, is experienced in the present moment. When your thoughts are wandering you miss opportunities and moments to enjoy the beauty of living. You cannot possibly embrace every moment as there are daily tasks to do and errands to run. Do not get so caught up in your work you live in a world that only exists in your head. There is life to be enjoyed and appreciated.

Learn from your past and quit dwelling on it! Stop focusing on an imaginary future as this keeps you from creating it. Also, it is possible for you to be so happy in your inner world, of meditation or reading spiritual texts, you lose touch with the reality of life.

There must be a balance between attending to life and enjoying the moment. Right now, stop take a deep breath and look around. Be aware of what you see and the feelings going through your body. Today appreciate each moment as you learn the balance between work and play.

Enjoy the day.

Mary Ellen Ciganovich www.askmaryellen.com

Notice your thoughts

The mind is an immensely powerful part of your human body. It is powerful and difficult to control. You find yourself thinking in a certain way, you know this thought causes you trouble, yet it is difficult for you to stop. Too often you become sick or exhausted because of your beliefs. You believe flu season is coming and you have this "thought" you will become sick. After all it must be true you get sick during this season every year.

To create what you want in life, make an effort to harness the power of your mind and think differently. Use the power of your thoughts to be of service to your physical body. Become aware of your power to create physical health through your mind. Now, you can choose to create the rest of your life through using the power of your mental energy.

Today harness the power of your mind as you choose your thoughts to create your life.

Enjoy the day.

Mary Ellen Ciganovich www.askmaryellen.com

Make your community better

All of us are part of a community. Whether it is the community of our world, your country, your state, your area, or your neighborhood, in one way or another you are part of a community. It is your job to make your community better.

Every community is made better through the talents of their members. Consider what you have to offer and find ways to offer your talents to your community. There are so many ways you can help.

You can throw a get together for people to become acquainted. Possibly you have computer skills that can assist someone. Maybe you know organic gardening and want to begin a community garden or farmer's market.

On a larger scale, you could raise money for a charitable cause or begin an idea of your own to improve our society. You are never too young or too old to make a difference.

It is easy for you to get caught up in your own life and forget you have a responsibility to make your community, our world a better place.

Today decide to do something to make a difference.

Enjoy your day.

Mary Ellen Ciganovich www.askmaryellen.com

Balance your obligations

Try not to schedule to much on any given day as this will overwhelm you and drain your energy.

Keeping this kind of schedule for any length of time will leave you feeling drained. Even when you enjoy your obligations, you must stay balanced.

There is a skill to balancing your obligations. First become aware of the many obligations on your schedule. Can you delete any that you do not enjoy or move one or two to a day when you schedule is not so crowded? Do you have more energy in the morning and less in the late afternoon? If so, schedule your activities accordingly.

Balance your life in such a way you do not have to miss opportunities. When you have a function, you must attend in the evening, plan ahead. You can oversleep in the morning or take a late afternoon nap.

Today remember you do not have to miss an opportunity; simply balance your obligations.

Enjoy the day.

Mary Ellen Ciganovich www.askmaryellen.com

95
Let go of the little things

Small frustrations or irritations hold power over you because they show you how you cannot control life. Every problem {misperception}, large or small, is a "life teacher." Every confusing situation is an opportunity to practice mindfulness. An irritating person gives you ac chance to practice compassion and empathy.

It is a sad fact "humans" tend to invest time and emotional energy in minor issues, attempting to avoid confronting major ones. You are looking left when you should be looking right. In other words, the "problem" you are focusing on is NOT the real problem. It is the issue your "ego" wants you to focus on to avoid dealing with your pain involved in the REAL problem.

Focusing on the small stuff provides you with a temporary sense of power and control. You might be able to fix this small problem. However, it is only after you let go of the little things that you realize your bigger problems are not so big after all. Today Let go of any small irritations or frustrations.

Enjoy the day.

Mary Ellen Ciganovich www.askmaryellen.com

Create unlimited possibilities

Keep an open mind and an optimistic outlook to see your many possibilities to create a meaningful life. An open mind helps you see any situation from a different point of view.

Consider all possibilities as you stretch your limits to strive forward. Let go of any preconceived societal teachings. As you adopt an attitude of optimism in ALL areas of your life, you attract opportunities for growth and learning. Open you mind going forward to see the many new opportunities in front of you.

Today welcome in a new realm of possibilities for success.

Enjoy the day.

Mary Ellen Ciganovich www.askmaryellen.com

Let go of anything holding you back

Within you is the ability to let go of things that held you back in the past. Take a deep breath, allow yourself to connect with your core strength. Release your fears of what others think. Become confident to freely express yourself.

Now, you are able to work through other past issues, learn and let go. Visualize these issues dissolving into nothingness as they float away. See your fears of being judged drop away as you stop judging others.

As you become attuned to the present moment, your fears melt, and you become open to living your Truth.

Today be honest with yourself as you utilize your present core strength to let go of past hurts.

Enjoy the day.

Mary Ellen Ciganovich www.askmaryellen.com

Grief is part of the human experience

As you experience anything causing you shock or sadness you may choose to withdraw from life. It is important to realize grief is part of the human experience.

During these difficult times, reach out to trusted, precious people who care about you. Rely on their strength to gather the nurturing you need. God speaks to you through many channels. As you open yourself up to receive God's messages you are able to deal with your grief productively. Grief is never easy as you feel raw and wounded at the same time.

Today trust in God to walk you through any sadness you may be dealing with in your life.

Enjoy the day.

Mary Ellen Ciganovich www.askmaryellen.com

Be open to receive

You must be open to accept what God gives you. When you approach life with your defenses up, you stop any desired outcomes you may want such as intimacy or unconditional love. Always be ready to receive your desires when they arrive.

Soften your barriers to allow these good feelings in when God presents them to you. Becoming receptive involves a softening of your defenses as well as a willingness to remain open to any new possibilities. First you must have within yourself the characteristic you want to receive. Example: If you want to receive love, first have love towards yourself. If you want to receive abundance, create the opportunities, and do the work to bring abundance into your life.

Today be clear about what you want to receive and first cultivate this characteristic within yourself.

Enjoy the day.

Mary Ellen Ciganovich www.askmaryellen.com

100
Be spontaneously delighted

Before you can be delighted with life, understand what makes you happy? What brings you joy? What do you do for fun? To many people have very vague answers for these extremely important questions. Life is way too short not to be enjoyed.

When you hear news that thrills you and makes you act spontaneously out of your joyfulness, stop to enjoy this feeling of joy! Express gratitude to God/The Universe for this joyful emotion. Listen to what your body is feeling so these feelings can be recreated. Stay in this joyful, happy moment relishing every second of happiness.

Through understanding these joyful moments and happy thoughts, you become closer to understanding yourself. You understand what you value, what excites you and what you no longer want in your life.

Living in the moment, staying NOW, means you are aware and fully engaged in life.

Today bring spontaneity to your life as you make every moment of your life full of joy!

Enjoy the day.

Mary Ellen Ciganovich www.askmaryellen.com

Connect with your inner Self

If you have trouble communicating your thoughts to other people, it may be a signal for you to turn within to clarify these thoughts. Spend time releasing scattered thoughts as you create a sense of calmness within you. You can now strengthen your relationship as you communicate clearly.

Find a quiet place to be alone as you release tensions. Turn your attention to your breath, as you breathe deeply from your spiritual center. Allow the power of silence to center and balance you. This strong connection to your inner Self enhances your connections to everyone around you.

When your thoughts are clear, and your emotions are calm you are able to communicate effectively with any person or relationship. It is usually your perception of the relationship that clouds your vision. Today fuel your connections with others by fostering a balanced, peaceful state of consciousness within yourself.

Enjoy the day.

Mary Ellen Ciganovich www.askmaryellen.com

102
Choose an attitude of joy

You may be in the habit of allowing your surroundings to determine your mood. This can be a hard habit to break until you become aware of what you are doing. Understand your mood can affect your environment in a positive way. You have the ability to choose.

Ask friends to help you spread joy and happiness. You and your friends can spread joy to others as you go about your day, or they can help you organize and get rid of clutter. Together your happiness is multiplied as all of you enjoy being playful. This inspires you and your friends to stay focused in a positive direction.

Choosing an attitude of joy empowers you to turn any environment into a positive one. Set an intention for your day to keep this joyful attitude no matter what happens around you.

Today inspire others as you create an attitude of joy.

Enjoy the day.

Mary Ellen Ciganovich www.askmaryellen.com

Overcome challenges

By keeping a clear mind and a strong sense of confidence in your abilities you can overcome any obstacle life throws your way.

First, look at this life challenge objectively. Let go of any fear-based thoughts you have surrounding it. Use your creative mindset to see all parts of the "problem." It is a misperception and with determination you can see things differently.

Continue moving forward with confidence and an invigorating attitude to see a solution. Keep this "obstacle" in its proper perspective instead of being intimidated by it or giving up. Never give up as this is your enemy. Apply your sharp mental focus to see creative solutions to any challenge life gives you.

Brainstorming solutions, on a daily basis, gives you a giant push forward to find your solution.

Today use a mindset of encouraged confidence to focus on dissolving any obstacles you face.

Enjoy the day.

Mary Ellen Ciganovich www.askmaryellen.com

You are love

It is part of your humanness that at times makes you doubt your self-worth. You question how important you are to the people in your life. Perhaps you even feel ignored or underappreciated in your personal life. This may lead you to go on a spending spree in an effort to feel better. Spending money to medicate your emotions is a wrong choice. Eventually this choice makes you feel worse.

You must look within to find validation and self-worth. As you look within you will see a generous loving person. Composed by love, to bring love and to give love back to our world. You are valuable and matter to our world, your friends, and your family. There is a source of endless love inside each of us, from this "well of love" you can all drink till your heart's content.

Today look within yourself to find the loving generous person you already are.

Enjoy the day.

Mary Ellen Ciganovich www.askmaryellen.com

Learn and grow through difficult times

It can be challenging to keep a positive attitude and a measure of faith during a difficult time. This is because during any difficult time your negative mindset kicks in creating more worrisome thoughts. As you become aware of these negative thoughts you can let go of them. This enables you to choose new positive ones.

Life is full of challenges. It doesn't matter what year it is, how old you are or your occupational level, there are always difficulties. Every day and every year of your life brings you a life challenge to learn about yourself.

It will help you to remember your life is just one phase after another. Any difficult time will give way to something new and different.

Today comfort yourself by repeating the wise saying, "this too shall pass."

Enjoy the day.

Mary Ellen Ciganovich www.askmaryellen.com

Empower yourself to lead

As you take leadership roles seriously, you empower yourself to make a positive difference in the lives of everyone you touch. It may be risky for you to accept a position of authority due to your fear of not being capable of successfully guiding others. When you do your best with the skills you have and you support others to make the most of their skills, your efforts will be met with positive outcomes.

Focus on being personally accountable to yourself as you commit yourself to leading others. As these people approach you with questions or advice treat them with respect and dignity. This is an important characteristic of being a good leader.

Today as you become a leader equip others to realize their ambitions.

Enjoy the day.

Mary Ellen Ciganovich www.askmaryellen.com

Treat yourself with care

As you go about your day, you may feel worried, tired, or anxious due to your concerns about the outside world. You may even feel like not leaving home at all. These emotions are normal. They are telling you to get some much-needed rest.

Stop feeling pressure to succeed or do more than you can possibly do in one day. These pressures, you put on yourself, leave you feeling worn down, stressed, and worried. Consider relaxing outside with a good book, getting a massage, pedicure, or manicure. Treating yourself gently and with care is a wonderful way to alleviate your concerns.

When you take time for yourself, treating yourself with patience, compassion and understanding you are showing God/The Universe you have respect for your body and mind.

Today gently nurture yourself to cope with the world more easily.

Enjoy the day.

Mary Ellen Ciganovich www.askmaryellen.com

Be honest with yourself

It is not possible for you to be in an honest relationship when you cannot assess yourself honestly. Your relationship is a mirror for you, first ask yourself," what do I need to work on within myself?" Be completely honest with yourself so you can understand why you are drawn to certain individuals and repelled by others.

Any relationship you are in should add value to your life experience. When you honestly understand yourself, you see the good qualities you value and want in any personal relationship.

Maintaining a mindfulness connection is hard and takes daily discipline to achieve. It is a valuable tool toward building a healthy relationship. You always feel better knowing your best relationships are a reflection of your heart's landscape.

Today be honest with yourself as you effectively navigate your personal relationships.

Enjoy the day.

Mary Ellen Ciganovich www.askmaryellen.com

Be passionate about living

As you become passionate about life, you find a multitude of experiences opening up for you. Your passion overtakes your soul and stimulates your other senses.

Look for beautiful sights, sounds and smells because as you do this your passion for life is ignited. Eat unfamiliar foods, try new activities, surround yourself with beauty as you enjoy being sociable.

Your passion for these new and pleasurable experiences is your guide to open your awareness level in your life. As you become eager, every day, to broaden your life experiences, you open the door to all of life's pleasures.

Today be passionate about life as you appreciate all the wondrous beauty our world has to offer.

Enjoy the day.

Mary Ellen Ciganovich www.askmaryellen.com

Make your movements mindful

When your thoughts are scattered it becomes difficult for you to focus on your many responsibilities. Life's unpredictability can trigger many tensions. If you find yourself in this predicament, take time to center yourself before continuing your day.

Centering yourself can be achieved in many ways depending on what works for you. You can journal, take a walk, or go to a local park. It may seem like an oxymoron and productive physical activity like exercise, house or yard work can ease your tensions and improve your focus.

Exercise frees the body and mind by using repetitive movements to soothe your mind. Your thoughts are now free to clear your mind.

Today use regular exercise and mindful movements to allow your thoughts to freely focus therefore quieting your mind.

Enjoy the day.

Mary Ellen Ciganovich www.askmaryellen.com

Feelings are not permanent

You can become overwhelmed by your feelings or emotions when you do not understand how to cope with these misunderstood feelings. Your feelings are never permanent. Allow these feelings to guide you to what you need to learn about yourself.

To help you become unattached to the effects your feelings have on your body, quietly sit down to simply let them be with no judgment of why you should or should not feel this way.

While your feelings may seem important at the time, they do NOT define you or your life. You can make the choice to keep these negative feelings. You can make the choice to allow these negative feelings to make you sick. If you make either of the following choices, you will stay stuck allowing life to pass you by.

Sadness, negative emotions, or any fear-based feeling is a signal for you to look within. Take a break from the rest of the world to find peace within yourself. Be aware of what you need to learn as you visualize these negative feelings melting away.

Today cope with any situation or feeling by knowing it is only temporary when you learn and let go.

Enjoy the day.

Mary Ellen Ciganovich www.askmaryellen.com

Choose, experience, learn and choose again

Never take life seriously. Life is about choosing, experiencing, learning, and choosing again. Your life experiences are perceptions or misperceptions. Focus on the NOW moment – the experience. What did you learn? How did/do you feel? Did you make the world, our society just a little bit better? Did you take the time to make one person's life better?

Even when events (things) in your life do not turn out as expected it is a gift in disguise. You probably will not know this at the time – it might take years for you to see how God has woven His plan for you.

Today appreciate your failures as you choose to learn something about yourself from the experience.

Enjoy the day.

Mary Ellen Ciganovich www.askmaryellen.com

Connect to the Universal laws – God's Laws – of Truth

It is important for you to realize you are a co-creator with the Universe/God when you allow this Universal energy and knowledge to flow through you. Use your intuitions – Knowing's – to guide you. As you understand these Universal Truths, and use them in your life, your serene sense of peace will inspire others to connect with God's Universal Truths as well.

It is always a good feeling when others agree with you, however you are only partially responsible as God/the Universe is working through you to send His messages to whomever you touch.

Today connect yourself to God's Universal Laws of Truth by allowing your intuitions – your knowing's – to guide you.

Enjoy the day.

Mary Ellen Ciganovich www.askmaryellen.com

Explore your past ONLY to navigate your future

To fully understand your future, be sure you know where you have been. Did you learn everything you needed to learn from your past errors? Consider all the issues you left unexplored because you made a choice to "hope" they would go away and leave you alone.

If you ever made this type of "choice" you understand the errors from your past that you did not learn from do not go away. When you do not learn from an error you hinder your efforts to evolve into the person you are meant to become.

You can understand how to create a more fulfilling life journey by exploring your unresolved issues and choosing to learn. Consider the choices you made in the past to gain a better understanding of the choices you want to make in the future. What do you want to achieve? What makes you genuinely happy?

As you explore these areas you empower yourself to make choices to benefit you in the present and future.

Today explore your past to learn as you enter a new phase of life.

Enjoy the day.

Mary Ellen Ciganovich www.askmaryellen.com

Elevate your consciousness

Your desire to help everyone feel as good as you do about a particular product/item or service is fine. Did you ever stop to think that some people do not need or want whatever service is making you feel so good? Just because something works for you does not mean it will have the same effect on other people.

Your mission in life is to elevate your consciousness. There is only one person whom you need to control, and that person is YOU! There is only one person who can make you happy, and that is YOU!

During any year, any month or any week concentrate on mastering your own self. Stop trying to blame other people. Stop trying to fix other people. Stop looking to other people to make you happy. Make yourself happy first! Fix your errors to learn and blame no one!

Today make it your mission in life to elevate your consciousness.

Enjoy the day.

Mary Ellen Ciganovich www.askmaryellen.com

Never forget how powerful your words are

It is up to you to make sure your word is sacred. When you make a promise go out of your way to keep your word.

People who keep promises are regarded as people of integrity while those who do not keep their promises are known as people who are not to be taken seriously. Promises not kept lead to disappointment and distrust. Even when it is a promise you make to yourself, it is important to follow through or your self confidence and self-esteem will suffer.

If it is not possible to keep a promise, go to the person and offer an alternative. Ask for forgiveness as you make other plans with them. Do the same ritual with promises you make to yourself. Ask yourself for forgiveness for a promise you no longer wish to hold on to. Then let go.

Today clear your conscience and know you are only as good as your word.

Enjoy the day.

Mary Ellen Ciganovich www.askmaryellen.com

Regularly center yourself

Take time throughout your day to regularly center yourself. Especially when you lose your focus of feel overwhelmed, take a short break to balance yourself as you visualize reenergizing yourself. Take time for a quick snack or cup of coffee as you reconnect with your spirit.

The time you take for yourself is valuable because it reignites your focus to manage multiple tasks with enthusiasm. Without this focus on your sense of purpose, your attention and thoughts become scattered in all directions.

As you center yourself, you take control of your focus and apply this focus in a structured way to become productive. You feel energized, busy, and grounded as you go about your day.

Today center your thoughts to channel your energy while staying grounded.

Enjoy the day.

Mary Ellen Ciganovich www.askmaryellen.com

An overly sensitive mood causes you to anger or react

Choose to respond rather than react to any situation especially if you find yourself becoming overly sensitive. Remain aware of your feelings. What is really going on within you? Is this a past painful situation coming back to teach you?

Do not take what others say and do personally. You never know what is going on in their day. Maintain an upbeat mood regardless of how other people choose to behave. Detaching from other people's behaviors or opinions helps you to understand their negativity has nothing to do with you. Take a step back to ask yourself," what do I need to learn from seeing this?"

Today choose to take control of any situation – RESPOND!

Enjoy the day.

Mary Ellen Ciganovich www.askmaryellen.com

Organize your thoughts

With the busy, active lives all of you live it is easy to feel overwhelmed by the many tasks and details you need to remember. Organizing your thoughts will free your mind.

The human brain has the potential to store massive amounts of information. It is the fast pace, in which you live your life, that hinders you from recalling information when it is needed.

As you set aside time to focus and organize your thoughts in a tangible way, you feel lighter and less mentally cluttered by unnecessary thoughts.

Today create order in your mind before you begin your task.

Enjoy the day.

Mary Ellen Ciganovich www.askmaryellen.com

Happiness is possible when you choose it

You can be happy all the time as long as you are happy with what you already have. Happiness tends to come and go through time as your ego allows it. With your ego self out of the way, happiness is yours at any moment.

Sadly, at times, external events tend to get in the way of choosing happiness. Things such as an illness, a death, or any tragedy you see on the news are all "stoppers" to happiness. These all make up part of the human experience. It is normal to be unhappy with such events. The tragic part of life is when you allow these events to stop your happiness for years to come.

Today choose to be happy knowing you cannot control anyone or anything.

Enjoy the day.

Mary Ellen Ciganovich www.askmaryellen.com

What you get when you achieve your goal is not as important as what you become when you achieve your goal.

Go forward living in Truth and inspiring our world.

Sincerely with love,

Mary Ellen Ciganovich

A personal note from Mary Ellen

Thank you for reading "Truth Lives." It is my dream for you to spread these Truths throughout the world. These are not my words; they are God's Universal Truths.

Each and every one of us are here to aid in the healing of our planet. All of us are here to make the world just a little bit better than when we arrived.

We have a purpose to love one another, be kind to each other, encourage each other, inspire each other, and motivate each other to be our best possible selves.

Can we all come together through the passion God gives us, the passion that lives in our hearts and souls to heal our planet?

I will do what I can.

Will you join me?

Sincerely with love,

Mary Ellen Ciganovich

Any questions about "Truth Lives" may be directed to

Mary Ellen Ciganovich

www.askmaryellen.com

PMB 573 Ooltewah, Tennessee 37363

Mec222@aol.com

About the Author

Mary Ellen Ciganovich is an avid writer of truth. She writes about Truth because she knows "Truth" will aid our world in the healing of our planet.

She was born in New York and raised in Atlanta, Georgia. Mary Ellen graduated Magna Cum Laude in Education from the University of Georgia. She is a life-long member of the Alpha Chi Omega sorority.

As a child Mary Ellen's family life was very dysfunctional as there were many fights between her parents. Mary Ellen turned to God, His Angels and prayer for support during these difficult times.

At the age of six, Mary Ellen was diagnosed with Epilepsy. Although it was a mild case of Petite Mal Temporal Lobe epilepsy, her parents taught her to hide this diagnosis from everyone. She was told over and over again what she couldn't do and with the power of God behind her Mary Ellen went forward to succeed.

After graduating from the University of Georgia, Mary Ellen married, had a daughter, and went on to teach middle school. In 1987, after her husband left, Mary Ellen moved back to the Atlanta area to raise her daughter.

During this time in Atlanta, Mary Ellen played tournament racquetball to get her hurtful emotions out in a positive way. As she played racquetball, Mary Ellen would become extremely hot, lose her balance, and walk as if drunk. She developed a sharp pain in her right eye that became debilitating.

Mary Ellen went to her neurologist. She was diagnosed with Multiple Sclerosis. The year was 1986. At that time there were no medications and almost no therapies for Multiple Sclerosis so Mary Ellen took it upon herself to find a healing that would work for her.

Mary Ellen always considered herself close to God. She knew He would lead her to find whatever she needed to learn from this diagnosis. She was determined NOT to be a "victim" of her MS monster!

The Atlanta Awareness Center became Mary Ellen's next stop on her journey. She knew the Bible is our greatest healing tool and Mary Ellen wanted to expand her spiritual knowing's. The Center taught spirituality through "A Course in Miracles." This powerful tool along with The Bible, prayer, meditation, Ayurvedic Healing therapies, herbs, vitamins, a lot of exercise and a strict diet has kept Mary Ellen's MS monster in his cave – most of the time!

Mary Ellen uses her teaching talents to assist many clients on their life journeys. "Truth Lives" is her third book in her Truth series and probably not her last! Her other books, "T.R.U.T.H. Taking Responsibility Unleashes True Healing" and "Healing Words, Life Lessons to

Inspire" can both be found on Amazon or through her website at https://www.askmaryellen.com

Mary Ellen and her husband Peter reside outside Chattanooga, Tennessee. Mary Ellen posts a "Truth of the day" on most all social media sites. These "Truths of the day" are also heard through Cyrus Webb's Conversations Live Radio news network and WYAD FM in Mississippi.

You can email her at askmaryellen@aol.com or write her at

R.E.A.L. Health - PMB 573 – Ooltewah, Tennessee 37363